Danger Colors

Grateful acknowledgement is made to:
G.I. Bernard: pages 5 (top), 7,12, 13 (bottom), 14, 15, 17, 21, 23, 29 (bottom) and title page
Waina Cheng: page 8
John Cheverton: page 16
Dr. J.A.L. Cooke: pages 5 (bottom), 13 (top left), 19, 20 (top), 22 (bottom), 29 (top)
Stephen Dalton: page 25 (bottom) and back cover
Fredrick Ehrenström: page 28
Michael Fogden: pages 9 (top), 11 (top), 22 (top), 26 and front cover.
Rudie H. Kuiter: page 10
Mantis Wildlife Films OSF: pages 11 (bottom), 27 (bottom)
Oxford Scientific Films: pages 9 (bottom), 18
Kjell B. Sandved: page 25 (top)
P and W Ward: pages 4, 6, 13 (top right), 20 (bottom), 24, 27 (top)

Originated and published in Great Britain by
Andre Deutsch Limited, 1986.
Printed and bound by Proost, Turnhout, Belgium
Library of Congress Cataloging-in-Publication Data
Danger colors.
   Summary: Text and illustrations introduce the characteristics of a variety of animals whose coloration protects them from their enemies.
   1. Protective coloration (Biology) — Juvenile literature.   [1. Protective coloration (Biology)]
I. Oxford Scientific Films.   II. Title.
QL767.D36   1986   591.57'2   86-637
ISBN 0-399-21341-4
G. P. Putnam's Sons, 51 Madison Avenue,
New York, New York 10010
First Impression

Millipede

Danger Colors

Oxford Scientific Films

edited by

JENNIFER COLDREY and KAREN GOLDIE-MORRISON

G. P. Putnam's Sons, New York

RED AND BLACK

Animals which are striped or spotted with red and black are usually poisonous or nasty to eat. Hungry enemies soon learn to avoid them.

Cinnabar Moth. A bird will be sick if it tries to eat this moth, which is beautiful, but poisonous.

Tree-hoppers. This group of red and black tree-hoppers, adults and babies together, is more frightening to a bird than one tree-hopper by itself.

Black Widow Spider. This red and black spider has a very venomous bite.

YELLOW AND BLACK

If birds, snakes or lizards try to eat these bright yellow and black animals, they will get sick. They soon learn not to touch other black and yellow animals.

Cinnabar Moth caterpillars. Birds and other animals which eat caterpillars will easily spot this large group of brightly colored, very poisonous caterpillars.

Arrow-poison Frog. A frog with a poisonous yellow and black skin doesn't have to worry about being eaten.

RED, YELLOW AND BLACK
The colors red, yellow and black also warn of hidden poisons.

Red-leg Grasshopper. An ant which moves too close to this grasshopper will get a blast of foul foam in its face. Next time, these bright colors will remind the ant to keep away.

Coral Snake. These bold patterns can be seen in the dark and they warn off mammal enemies, such as agouti, which hunt at night.

Pajama Sea Slug. Poisonous sea slugs can show off their fabulous colors without being bothered.

OTHER COLORS
Blues, greens and blacks sometimes signal danger.

Blue-ringed Octopus. The vivid blue rings are a clear warning that this octopus is poisonous. One bite can kill a person.

Arrow-poison Frog. These metallic colors signal danger.

Snout Beetle. This jewel-like beetle has a hard body which makes it difficult to eat.

WASPS AND THEIR IMITATORS

Wasps have stingers and are striped black and yellow. Birds as well as people soon learn not to touch them. Some harmless insects imitate the wasp's coloring to warn off their enemies which will think they can sting.

Common Wasp. The black and yellow stripes of a wasp signal its nasty sting.

Wasp Beetle.

Clearwing Moth.

Hoverfly.

These three insects look like wasps, but none of them can sting. Which wasp copycat looks most like the real wasp to you?

BOGUS BUMBLEBEES

Bees have stingers and fat, hairy bodies. Birds and people soon learn not to touch them. Harmless insects copy this shape and coloring to pretend that they too will sting and hurt.

Red-tailed Bumblebee. The fat and hairy, black and red body of this bee warns of its nasty sting.

Hoverfly. This harmless hoverfly has a fat and hairy, black and red body just like the red-tailed bumblebee. It also buzzes, but it cannot sting.

LADYBUG LOOK-ALIKE

When touched, ladybugs produce a foul-smelling yellow liquid from their leg joints. Birds, other beetles and spiders learn from experience not to touch ladybugs or other red and black beetles.

Ladybug.
This ladybug is red with black spots.

16

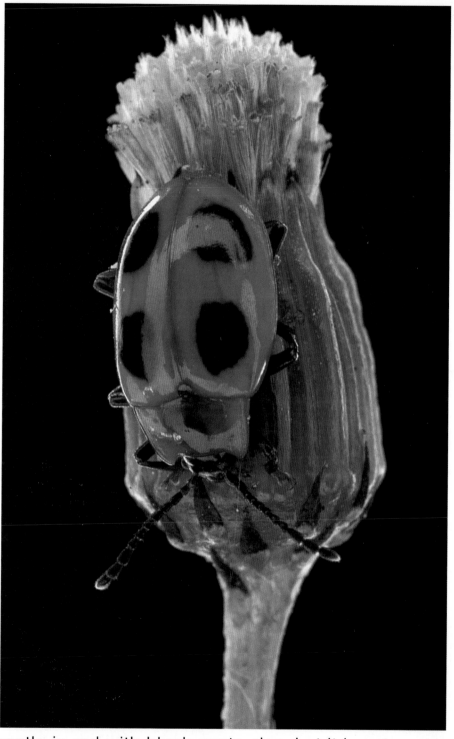

Fungus Beetle. This beetle is red with black spots also, but it is not nasty to eat. Its enemies confuse it with the ladybug and won't touch it.

ANT PROTECTION

Ants can either bite or sting and larger animals usually leave them alone.

Ant. Ants don't stay still very long. They scurry about looking for food. They have narrow waists and six legs.

Jumping Spider. Birds and lizards often hunt spiders but they leave this spider alone. Can you tell why?

Baby Mantid.
This mantid also looks like an ant, but it cannot bite or sting.

BLUFFERS

Many insects hide from their enemies. But some, when alarmed, suddenly "make faces" or wave brightly colored tails in the air. This scares away the intruders.

Puss Moth caterpillar. This caterpillar looks like a rolled leaf, but must keep still or it may be discovered...

...A bird has disturbed the caterpillar. It must now scare away the bird or else be eaten, so it becomes a red-faced monster.

Forest Moth. This dull, blackish moth resembles a dead leaf on the mossy forest floor.

But if it is touched, it opens its wings suddenly, arches its body and shows off its hairy red-and-black banded body and yellow tail.

STARTLERS

A sudden flash of bright color often frightens away an enemy.

Stump-tailed Skink. This lizard looks fierce with its red mouth wide open and its foaming blue tongue sticking out.

Ring-neck Snake. This snake is brown like the ground around it. But when it is alarmed it flicks over its coils and waggles its red tail.

Fire-bellied Toad.
This toad looks
rather dull and
colorless most of
the time until it
senses danger…
Suddenly it flips over onto its back displaying its red and black spotted
belly in an attempt to stop the snake from attacking.

EYE-OPENERS

The eyes of birds, mammals and snakes are all large and round and can frighten other animals. Many harmless butterflies and moths have false eyes on their wings so that their enemies will mistake them for these large animals.

Eyed Hawk-moth. This moth rests with its front wings covering the back wings and looks like a withered and crumpled leaf.

When alarmed, the moth snaps its front wings upwards and two large round eyes stare out from its back wings.

Hawk-moth. Another pair of bold eyes with which to frighten a threatening bird.

Owl Butterfly. This false eye looks real. What animal has eyes that look like this?

SNAKE COPYCATS

Many snakes have poisonous fangs or can suffocate their prey. Small harmless animals sometimes try to look like snakes to terrify their attackers.

Palm Viper. This snake is waiting quietly in the jungle for its next meal. All animals are frightened of this poisonous snake.

Caterpillar. This animal is obviously a caterpillar, but it is a caterpillar imitating a snake by blowing up its front end to show two large pretend eyes.

If you were a bird in the jungle and suddenly noticed these large eyes staring at you, what would you do?

HEADS OR TAILS?

Hunting animals usually strike at the head of their prey, taking aim at the eyes. Animals with a false head may escape death or severe injury when they are attacked.

Four-eye Butterfly Fish. It is easy to see one large false eye in this picture. Where are the other three eyes? And where is the real head?

Imperial Blue.
This butterfly has false feelers on the tip of its back wings which are more noticeable than the real ones.

Slug Caterpillar.
If you were a bird, which end would you go for?

MORE FACTS

RED AND BLACK (pages 4-5)

Cinnabar Moth. Unlike most moths, cinnabars fly about during the day without fear of being eaten because their bodies contain poisons. This is the adult of the yellow and black caterpillars on page 6.

Tree-hoppers. Protected by their danger colors, these tree-hoppers feed openly. The large group reinforces the warning signal. The picture shows adults and young: the adults have an enlarged, protective thorax; the young do not.

Black Widow Spider. Variously called "redback" or "button spider," the black widow spider is found in warm countries from the United States to New Zealand. The bite can kill a child or an old person, but seldom a healthy adult. The amount of red varies from country to country.

YELLOW AND BLACK (pages 6-7)

Cinnabar Moth caterpillars. They feed unconcealed in large groups which reinforces the warning to birds and other animals. The toxins are absorbed from ragwort, a highly poisonous food plant, which they eat. These are the caterpillars of the adult moth on page 4.

Arrow-poison Frog. The skin glands of these tiny South American frogs produce poisons which are so repulsive that a predator, such as a snake or bird, quickly spits them out. The frog usually escapes unharmed and the predator learns its lesson. The frogs are active during the day. Local Indians collect and concentrate the poison for use on their arrows.

RED, YELLOW AND BLACK (pages 8-9)

Red-leg Grasshopper. The foam is squirted from the leg joints. Brilliantly colored grasshoppers are more sluggish than camouflaged ones. In flight, the brightly colored back wing is conspicuous. They live in areas of sparse vegetation (Solomon Islands) and feed on toxic plants.

Coral Snake. "Coral" comes from the colors, not from an association with coral reefs. These very poisonous snakes burrow in soil and leaf litter, and feed on lizards, snakes, frogs and young birds. They may be uncovered by any mammal rooting in the soil, day or night. When threatened, the tail mimics the normal darting movements of the body, drawing the predator or prey's attention away from the snake's head which can then make a surprise strike.

Pajama Sea Slug. It is found in coral reefs in the Indo-Pacific, and feeds on invertebrates. Special glands produce the distasteful secretions, which make any fish spit out the sea slug.

OTHER COLORS (pages 10-11)

Blue-ringed Octopus. It is a small octopus, the size of an adult palm. It normally blends in with its background on reefs and under stones, around Australasia, and the vivid blue rings appear when it is disturbed or is eating. It takes only a second for the octopus to display its warning rings.

Arrow-poison Frog. See Yellow and Black.

Snout Beetle. If a predator ignores the colors and attacks, this Papua New Guinea beetle draws in its legs and antennae, drops to the ground and stops moving. This is another way it can escape danger.

WASPS AND THEIR IMITATORS (pages 12-13)

Wasp copycats include various moths, beetles, flies and other stingerless wasps and bees.

Wasp Beetle. The wasp beetle is striped black and yellow like a wasp. It also has a wasp-like shape, and when it moves it imitates a wasp by scurrying about in the sunshine, continually moving its antennae, and even buzzing if disturbed.

Clearwing Moth. Not only does this moth copy the wasp's colors, but its wings are also wasp like. Unlike most moths, this moth's wings have very few scales and are transparent. Many moths are active at night, but the clearwings fly about by day without fear of being eaten.

Hoverfly. With its waspish coloring and shape, this hoverfly is easily mistaken for a wasp as it hovers and feeds from flowers. It has only one pair of wings, while wasps have two. Many other hoverflies mimic wasps and bees.

BOGUS BUMBLEBEES (Pages 14-15)

Red-tailed Bumblebee. Once a bee stings, it dies because the poison sacs are pulled out of its body with the stinger. This bee is a worker collecting nectar and pollen for the nest. Bees have four wings.

Hoverfly. This species exists in several different forms, each mimicking a different species of bee. Like all flies they have only two wings, unlike bees which have four. They hover near bumblebee nests without fear of being attacked

ust waiting for the chance to deposit their larvae
n the nest with the bumblebee eggs.

ADYBUG LOOK-ALIKE (pages 16-17)

adybug. When offered to captive birds,
adybugs are ignored or rejected. The yellow
quid tastes awful and can cause skin rashes in
eople. Because they are hard and smooth,
adybugs are also hard to grasp.
ungus Beetle. These beetles are commonly
ound in family groups, under tree bark or in
ungi.

NT PROTECTION (pages 18-19)

nt. An ant sting hurts because it contains a
quid of formic acid. Workers outside the nest
nove about constantly, searching for food,
sually other insects, and communicating their
nds to fellow workers.
umping Spider. This spider is shaped like an
nt with a narrow waist, slender body and long
egs. All spiders have eight legs, but when the
umping spider stops moving it holds its front legs
orward and keeps them moving to imitate the
ibrating antennae of an ant. Only when this spid-
r jumps on an insect or trails a safety thread of
ilk, does it betray its true identity.
aby Mantid. These mantids look like ants only
vhen they are young. As they grow larger, the
nt disguise is lost, and most become camou-
aged like leaves or twigs. Mantids lie in wait for
ies, grasshoppers and caterpillars.

LUFFERS (pages 20-21)

uss Moth caterpillar. This caterpillar feeds at
ight and hides by day. Its green color is
ormally enough protection if it stays still. But if it
disturbed it "makes a face" that is generally
nough to startle the enemy so that it either
rops the caterpillar or hesitates long enough for
to escape. "Making a face" involves inflating
e head end to reveal the black "eyes" and
carlet face. At the same time it raises its head
nd tail end. If this is not sufficient to deter the
ttacker, the caterpillar extends two red filaments
om its forked tail and lashes them around. The
aterpillar's head end is also hard, which makes
difficult to grasp, and fear causes it to tighten
s grip on the twig.

Forest Moth. In addition to the warning display,
the bunch of yellow hairs at the end of its body
may release a pungent smell to deter predators.

STARTLERS (pages 22-23)

Stump-tailed Skink. In this threat display, the
lizard arches its body, hisses and opens its
mouth wide and sticks out its tongue. It has
strong teeth but does not use them to bite,
merely to scare predators.
Ring-neck Snake. This snake, which is only ¼
inch thick and 15 inches long, is harmless. The
top side of the coils are brown and the underside
is bright red. The red tail mimics an open mouth
and can be mistaken for the head by an enemy.
The snake can then dart to freedom in the opposite direction.
Fire-bellied Toad. It relies on camouflage, but
resorts to a dramatic back flip if disturbed. At the
same time, an increased flow of poisonous skin
secretions makes it unpalatable and hard to hold.
Unfortunately for this one, grass snakes like the
taste of fire-bellied toads.

EYE-OPENERS (pages 24-25)

Eyed Hawk-moth. This moth is often seen at
dusk in the woods. It enhances the eye display
by moving up and down to look like an owl in its
nest hole. The moth has to rely on bluff because
it cannot fly away quickly. First it has to warm up
its flight muscles by shivering for several min-
utes. Predators probably relate the moth's eye
spots to the eyes of their own vertebrate
predators.
Hawk-moth. These are the convincing eyes on a
hawk-moth from New Caledonia.
Owl Butterfly. For an enemy, close-up and about
to attack, each bottom wing resembles part of the
face of an owl. If the "owl" eye startles the
predator, the butterfly may have time to escape.
The highlight spot to one side of the pupil pro-
duces an illusion of roundness. Apart from
eyespots, the butterfly is also well camouflaged.

SNAKE COPYCATS (pages 26-27)

Palm Viper. These snakes are extremely poisonous and well camouflaged. They coil around
tree stems, dangling head down in the tropical
forests of Costa Rica. The eyes are menacing.
Caterpillar. These caterpillars are usually well

camouflaged, but when threatened transform themselves into tiny snakes. The large pretend eyes mimic the menacing eyes of a poisionous viper. This caterpillar may look harmless to us, but it can scare off birds and other animals, who do not wait to see if it's a snake or not.

This disembodied head belongs to another snake-mimicking caterpillar, but a bird or small mammal is frightened off by its resemblance to a snake.

HEADS OR TAILS? (pages 28-29)

Four-eye Butterfly Fish. This fish has one real eye and one large false eye on each side of its body. The real eye is concealed within a stripe and seems small, while the false eye is large and conspicuous and near the tail. The more conspicuous ''eye'' draws a predator to the wrong end of the fish, which can then escape in the opposite direction.

Imperial Blue. This butterfly uses a bright orange patch and dark eyespots, in addition to false feelers, to create a false head. A bird is deceived into snapping at the false head and ends up with pieces of wing. Meanwhile the butterfly escapes with minor wing injuries. The disguise is enhanced when the butterfly is feeding. The false feelers twitch up and down like true antennae. Some butterflies even turn around on landing so that their false heads face the direction in which they were flying.

Slug Caterpillar. It is not easy to spot the head end because this caterpillar copies both the head's and tail's disguise to the full. It is also covered with stinging hairs and spines which can hurt. The hairs may also deter parasitic wasps from laying eggs in the caterpillar.